When I am old and in my rocking chair,

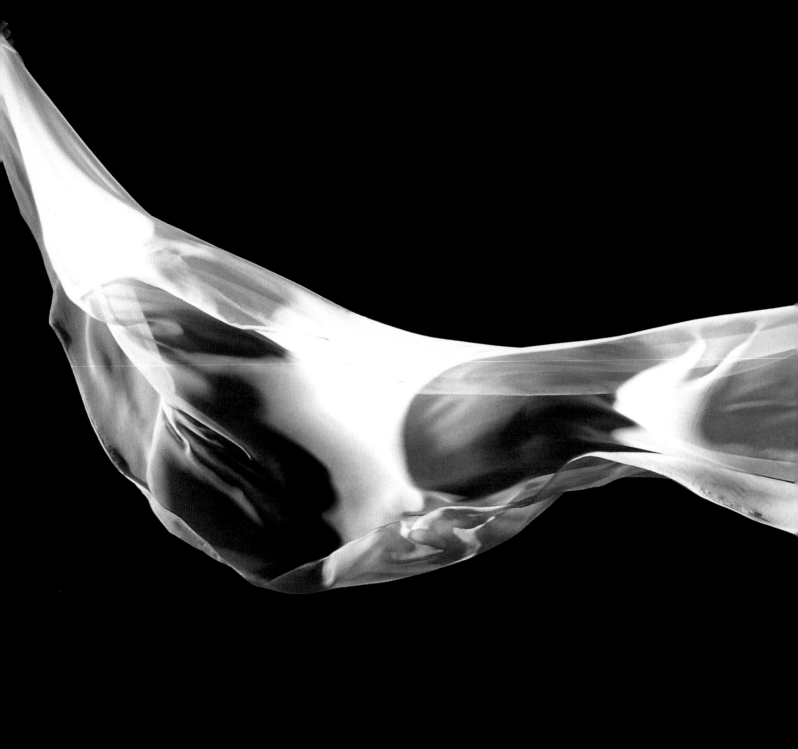

I don't want to
open my book and say
to my children
or my grandchildren,
"*Okay,*
I have this
World Championship
medal from 1993,
and I have this
Olympic gold medal
from 1994,"
end of story.

Of course I'm proud
of those achievements, but
I want to
open my book
and say...

a Flower.

It is not the scores or medals I want to remember, but my expression, the way I skated, the way I expressed myself.

Skating

OKSANA BAIUL

Compiled by

Christopher Sweet

with a foreword by

Dorothy Hamill

Original Photography by

Simon Bruty

Designed by **Alexander Isley Inc.**

Universe

Published in the United States
of America in 1997 by
UNIVERSE PUBLISHING
A Division of Rizzoli
International Publications, Inc.
300 Park Avenue South
New York, NY 10010

97 98 99 / 10 9 8 7 6 5 4 3 2 1

Library of Congress
Cataloging-in-Publication Data
Baiul, Oksana, 1977 or 8-
Secrets of Skating/Oksana Baiul;
Compiled by Christopher Sweet;
with original photography by
Simon Bruty; with a foreword by
Dorothy Hamill. p. cm.
ISBN 0-7893-0104-0 (hc)
1. Skating I. Sweet, Christopher.
II. Title. GV849.B.25 1997
796.91 '2'092--dc21
[B]   97-26039 xCIP

Printed in the United Kingdom

Contents

Foreword

The world of figure skating has changed enormously over the past few years. It has always been a sport that requires a unique balance of technical precision and artistry, but today, skating has become a world of remarkable intensity—one that requires the strength and endurance of the toughest sports and the sensitivity and grace of dance. Yet, as the ranks of top figure skaters become younger and younger and the required moves become more complicated, the emphasis on athleticism can often overshadow the less tangible aspects of a great skater's talent.

Earlier in this century, a very young Olympian, Sonja Henjie, captured the hearts of spectators the world over, and yet the young Norwegian might look rather out of place in today's competitive arenas. Not because she possessed less technical skill or artistic talent, but because, quite simply, so much more is done on the ice today. Many skating superstars have traveled down the trail that Sonja Henjie blazed three-quarters of a century ago, but few have succeeded in matching her exuberance and sense of line and grace.

There is a special way each skater carves the ice; it is as personal as a signature. It is a way of expressing who we are. To understand this, and to understand what goes into a great routine—and a great skater—you have to go beyond the rink. In this stunning volume, we discover Oksana Baiul's unique philosophy, and we see in her the reflection of the great skaters, like Sonja Henjie, that came before her. In words and captivating pictures, the secrets of this exacting profession are beautifully and elegantly brought to light through the perspective of one of the sport's very finest practitioners.

— *DOROTHY HAMILL*

IN RUSSIA, EVERYONE STARTS SKATING WHEN THEY ARE REALLY YOUNG. IT IS JUST THE WAY.

YOU HAVE TO START BY THE TIME YOU ARE FIVE YEARS OLD. OTHERWISE EVERY-BODY THINKS YOU ARE TOO OLD AND NOT GOOD ENOUGH TO START SOMETHING THAT TAKES AS MUCH DISCIPLINE AS SKATING. MY MOM WANTED ME TO BE A BALLET DANCER, BUT MY GRANDFATHER WANTED ME TO BE A FIGURE SKATER.

Mother and Daughter in Dnepropetrovsk

It turned out that I was not old enough to go to the ballet school, so my grandfather told my mom, "Listen, bring her to the ice rink." I was a little bit big for my age, and my grandfather said, "She will lose some weight and then she will go on to ballet school." And so instead of going to the ballet studio I went to the ice rink....

By the time I entered my first competitions, when I was seven years old, I realized I had talent. So when my mom finally asked me if I wanted to go to ballet school, I said, "Oh, no, I want to keep skating."

That's the story.

All my life
I had
guys as friends.
I didn't
play girl games;
I didn't
play with dolls.

I remember
when I was a kid,
we had nice rugs
at home,
and when my
mom was on the
telephone with
somebody—
of course,
she was really proud
of my skating
and she was saying
to her friends,
"Oh, Oksana is
skating and doing
really well"—
do you know
what
I was doing?

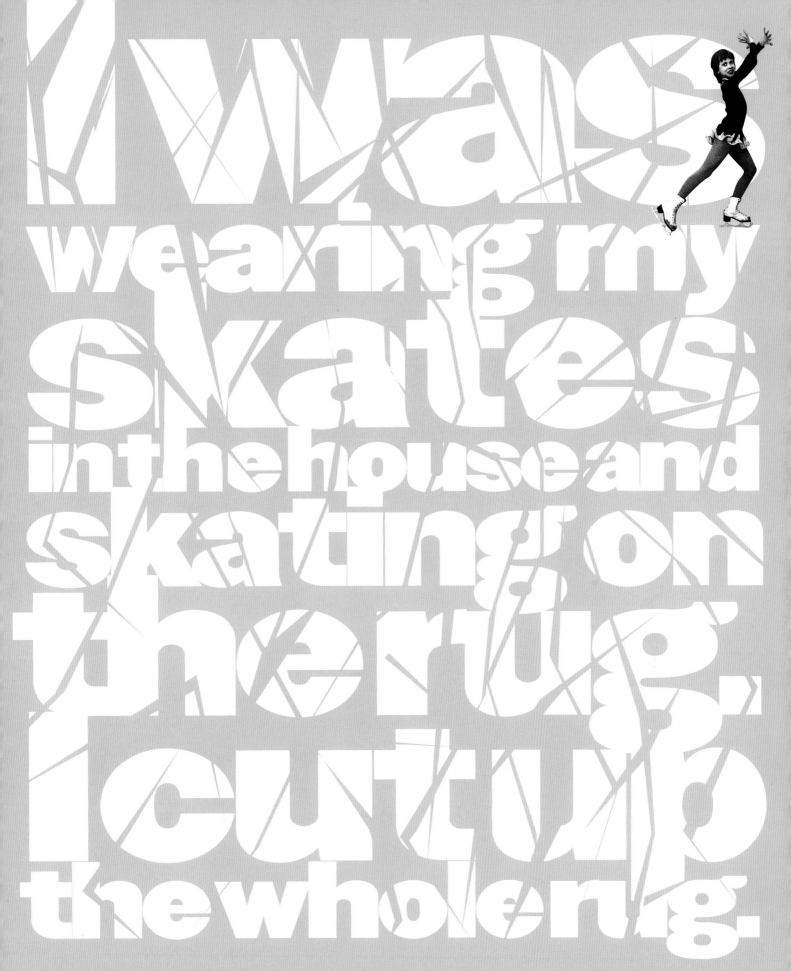

I was wearing my skates in the house and skating on the rug. I cut up the whole rug.

When she came into the room and saw it she almost had a heart attack.

We used to live on the third floor and I didn't have guards for my blades, or I would forget them somewhere, so I would put on my skates and walk on the cement up and down the stairs and back and forth to the rink near my house. And I would train after walking outside on my skates.

My mom was really tough on me at that time — really, really tough — because she wanted me to be a great student but still be great on the ice rink. I would wake up at six o'clock, have my first practice, and then go to school. In the afternoon, after school, I would go back to the ice rink for about two or three hours, six days a week.

At the beginning I was learning with others. In Russia we had big group lessons sponsored by the city.

At the
Dnepropetrovsk
Ice Rink

Like most everything, the skating program was part of our socialist system back then. Stanislav Korytek became my first serious coach when I was about seven or eight years old and I stayed with him until I was fourteen.

As a kid I didn't know I was better at skating than other kids. I was always skating in a group, but it was a group of five or six guys. I was the only girl. The guys were always pushing me to jump as well as they did. So when I went to competitions with girls, they said I was jumping like a guy.

When I was in junior competitions, I was often competing with girls five or six years older than me. There were a lot of kids in these groups, but then each group started getting smaller until I was the only one left, the only one competing at the higher and higher levels.

The balletic training that Oksana and most Russian skaters get at a young age is an absolutely essential part of their excellence. There seems to be a more tangible connection with the soul in all of Russian culture. Russian composers, novelists, ballet dancers, and skaters expose their souls in their work. The skaters, particularly the women, do this on the ice and display a much more somber, elemental feeling than other skaters do.

— *E. M. SWIFT*

One of the things
that first struck me about
her skating was the
limberness of her upper
body. She seemed like a
rubber band, like her upper
body could hit any shape,
and any time her arm went
overhead it would sort of
hyperextend. Really limber.
Very balletic.

—BRIAN BOITANO

The first time I saw the Olympics was on T.V. in 1988. Brian Boitano and Katarina Witt won the gold medals, and I remember my mom telling me, "Look at those skaters. Look how they are moving their arms." And I watched. The next year I couldn't take my eyes off Jill Trenary when she won the World Championships. Watching her, Galina would tell me: "Now that is figure skating." That was when I realized that figure skating is the only sport that makes athleticism so beautiful, so artful.

Later, when Jill was on tour with me in 1993 and in 1994, she looked out for me. I remember trying to look like her, to be like her, to communicate with her, to talk to her, and to understand her. I knew that I had to do my own thing, but just then I thought she was the most beautiful artist in the world. You could say I was a big fan.

Jill Trenary

It's like ballet, but on skates, but you can do much more on skates than you can just on your toes.

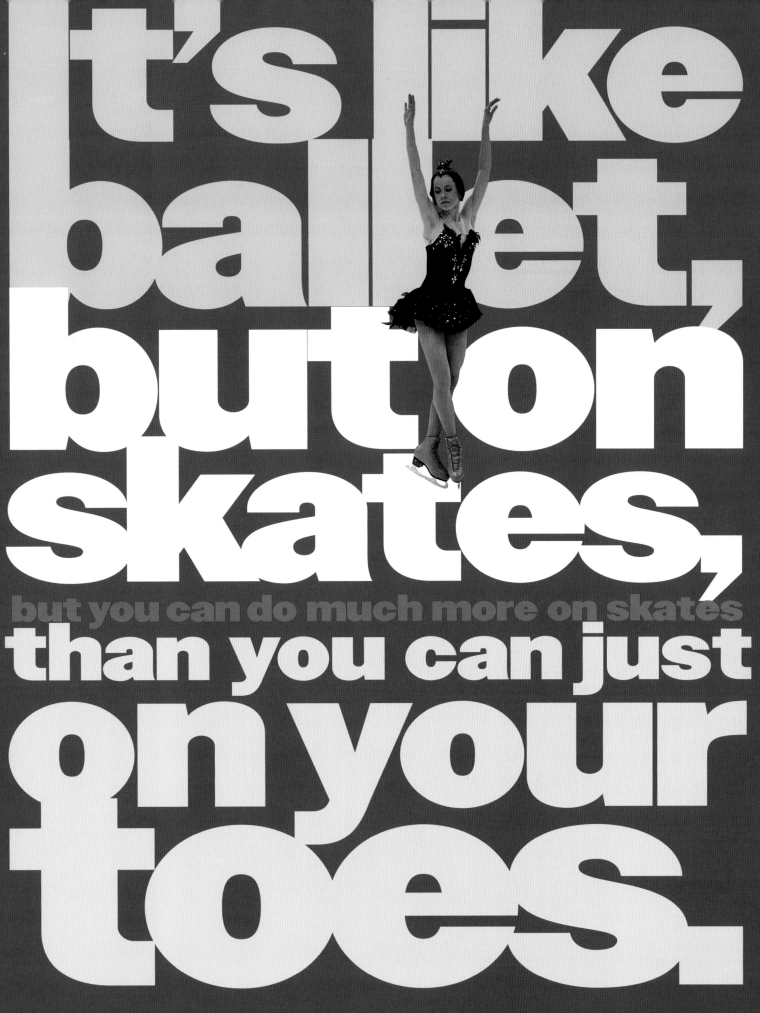

When I was about fourteen we had an important Junior Olympics competition. Stanislav Korytek was working with me then. My mom had died the year before that. I wasn't living with them, but Stanislav, his wife, and daughter were like a family to me. It was the last competition in the season and Stanislav couldn't come to the competition with me. When I returned, he wasn't there. I heard that he had gone to Canada and was not coming back. We were supposed to start training again. So I had to do something about my skating, and I was really angry.

I went to the director of the ice rink, handed in my skates, and said, "I don't want to skate anymore. My coach has left, and I am by myself. So I am going back to my stepfather, going back to school to be a normal kid." That's what I told him.

I started studying again, but all the time I was going to school I could see the ice rink in front of me. I started to realize that something was missing in my life. It was not my mother; it was not Stanislav.

It was ice.

It was skating.

So I went back to the rink.
I had thrown my boots
away, but I had
grown a little,
so I needed new ones anyway.
My stepfather
bought me another pair.
I started skating again,
but I was so out of shape.
That was the first time
I ever felt like that.
It had only been a few weeks but
I felt like something
was wrong with
my body.
So that September, I decided to
leave Dnepropetrovsk....

Beauty
is in the
details...

...preparing
for
competition

THE
AMATEUR
LIFE

Mastering the Sport

High honors:
with the
President
of Ukraine
after
Lillehammer

WHEN I WAS A KID
I NEVER
FELT LIKE
I WAS
GOOD
ENOUGH
TO GO TO THE
OLYMPICS.

I first heard about Oksana Baiul in January 1993. That was just before World Championships in Prague—which she would go on to win. I heard such glowing reports I just couldn't believe it. As she was described to me, I thought no skater could be that artistically gifted at such a young age. I thought that the person who told me about her must have been crazy, but then when I witnessed her performance a couple of months later in Prague, I went up to this person, apologized, and said that the description had been completely accurate.

—TOM COLLINS

Galina

I wanted to skate. And I realized that Dnepropetrovsk had a good school, but no great coaches. By then, I had already heard a lot about Galina Zmievskaya—that she was considered the top Russian figure skating coach and that she had trained Victor Petrenko, who had won the Olympic bronze in 1988 and was soon to win the gold. So I went to Odessa, where she was coaching. People have said that Victor Petrenko found me sleeping at their ice rink, but it's not true. I was staying at a friend's house. I had a lot of people around me all the time and my business was everybody's business. I went on my own to the rink at Odessa, but Galina wasn't there. She was with Victor on the Tom Collins tour in America, and her deputy coach, Valentine Nikolaj, was working with Galina's students in her absence. I introduced myself and asked if I could take lessons from him, and he said, of course.

When Galina came back from the tour, I was very scared. At the first practice, I started skating around, knowing she was somewhere up in the stands, watching carefully. By that time she had already told herself that she didn't want to teach anymore, that she was done with teaching, having trained Victor. She was already forty-eight years old. She had two daughters and just wanted to return to her village to rest and play with the kids. But—as she confessed to me much later—when she came to the ice rink and looked at me that day, she immediately changed her mind. At that first practice there were a lot of kids on the ice, but she called to me and asked me my name. Then she said to me, "Well, Oksana, you are a really talented kid. If it's okay with your parents, then I will start working with you." That's what she told me.

There were about eight or nine ten-to-fifteen-year olds in the group. Galina gave everyone an assignment. Students would take turns, and older students would help the younger ones. Galina was never in skates herself, but she watched all of us closely. A trainer-coach knows how to give specific skating assignments and make them fun, as though they are a game. And through these games and challenges, Galina inspired competition among the students and developed their sense of competitiveness. And when I fell, Galina would ask, in an almost harsh manner, "Why did you fall?" But inside, as the coach, she knew she was asking herself the same question.

—VICTOR PETRENKO

I WAS THIS KID WITH MY EYES S O  BIG BECAUSE SHE WAS A REALLY TOP COACH.

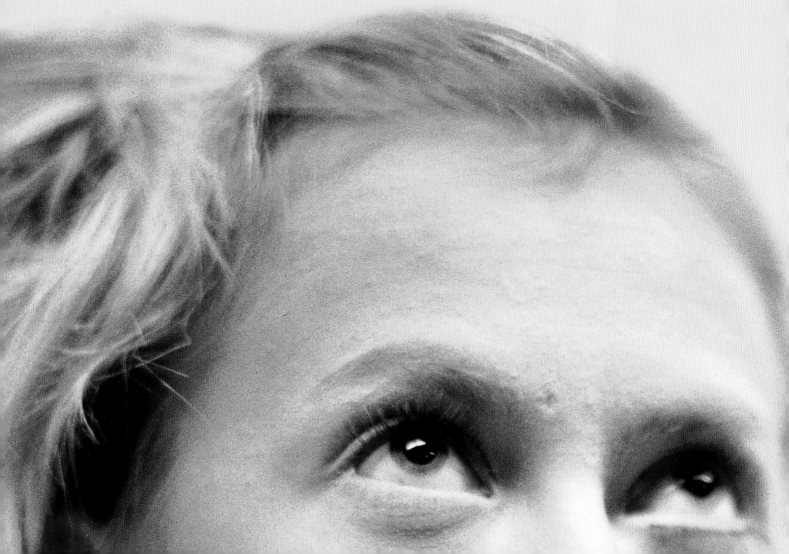

I skated off with the other kids, and Galina talked to Nikolaj, who knew a little bit about me, and she repeated that she wanted to talk to my parents. He told Galina that I had no parents, that my coach had left, that I had only my stepfather. The next day she took me into her family. Galina took care of me like a mother. I knew I had the best coach, but I knew I had to work really hard as well. She had to do so much for me at first. I remember we went to a competition in Germany, and it was my first competition at the international level. I could barely skate with the old boots I had. Galina looked at them, took me straight to a little shop by the rink, and bought me a new pair. She was able to take care of me, able to help me understand what was required without spoiling me. And that balance, that chemistry makes it happen. I felt myself getting better and better. And I kept thinking of my mother. When she was alive, she told me, "You have to be the best at whatever you do."

That same year, Ukraine separated from Russia. So my first major competition working with Galina was the Ukrainian championship, and I became our new country's first national champion.

Then in January 1993
I got second place in the

**Europeans
at Helsinki.**

And at the
Worlds, I came
in first.
That was my first
big year.

It all happened so quickly.

As a figure skater, you learn to live with injuries. I was injured in 1993 at the Worlds in Prague. During practice, Galina and Nikolaj had asked Katarina Witt to come over and meet me. I was so excited to be introduced to her that when I turned around and started skating away, my boot just caught the ice, and I fell down hard on my back. That was my first real injury—and right in front of Katarina, the two-time Olympic champion—but it was a sign of things to come, an omen. At the Olympic Games and at the Worlds I also skated with injuries. I began to take care of my body more seriously. As a skater, there are so many little things you have to watch out for, and you can't always avoid getting hurt.

With Katarina Witt, 1993

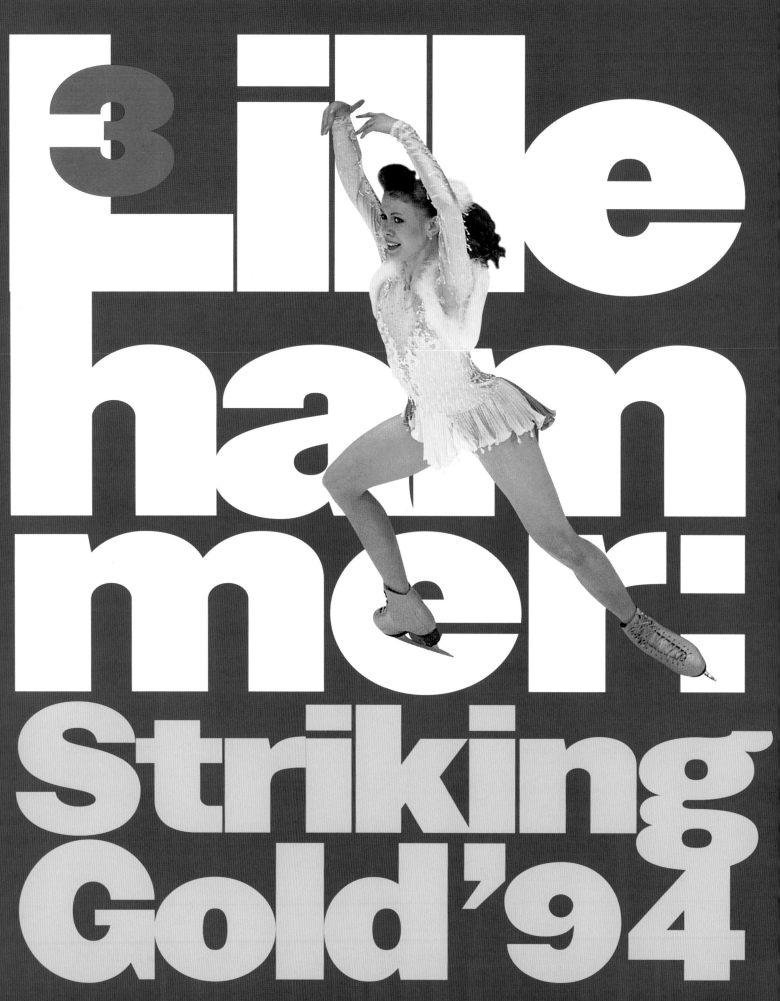

3 Lillehammer:
Striking Gold '94

During the years leading up to Lillehammer, I was working very hard, but I never felt like I had to win the Olympics, or Worlds, or anything. I just wanted to be the best skater for myself, and especially for my mother and my family.

An Olympic routine has to be very precise, but I think the main reason I won was that I was able to improvise and be flexible.

I remember after I completed the short program at Lillehammer, I was in second place and Nancy Kerrigan was in first. I was really happy with my position. Then we had a day off, and the day after that we would skate the free program. In the free program you have four minutes to do anything you want, but you have to do about six jumps to do well.

Then I had a really bad accident at the practice session on the day between programs. I was skating while Tanja Szewczenko, a German competitor, was skating. She was jumping on the right side, and I was jumping on the left side. She was going into a lutz and I was going into a lutz. I didn't look for her and she didn't see me. We collided at high speed, and I had to get three stitches in my leg, my back was hurting, and I could barely walk.

At that moment I felt I had been struck in my body, in my heart, and in my soul.

I was devastated. "Oh my God," I thought, "I am not going to be able to go through with it." The day after, Galina kept asking me how my back was feeling, and I kept insisting, without even thinking about it, "Yes, Galina, I'm okay." "Okay", she said, "Let's try to do a single axel. That is the easiest jump. Just do it as a warm up." I tried the jump but couldn't land it because it was so painful. I knew I had to skate my free program in the evening, and I was so upset I went straight to my room. I had been on a diet: I couldn't eat chicken; I couldn't eat this or that. But that afternoon, I went to the kitchen, the athlete's cafeteria, and filled up a plate bigger than a table. I ate chicken, I ate salmon—I tried everything. And it felt so good. Then I went back to my room and I slept.

Later, I woke up and went for a walk through Lillehammer, and it was so beautiful. After that I felt like my nerves, my whole body, were so comfortable. And I thought to myself...

I can do it. I can do it. I can do it...

A Gold-Medal Performance

When I got back to the rink, I said to Galina, "I feel like I can do it." I took a shower, put on my makeup, and went to the ice rink. I started to warm up on the floor. Then a doctor injected three or four shots into my back. We had six minutes each on the ice to warm up before the programs began, so I went onto the ice and had a really strong warmup. I did everything, every single triple jump, just like that—snap, snap, snap. And Galina was standing there with Victor; I can still see their faces—amazed. When I came over to them Galina would not talk to me. She didn't want to distract me. She just said, "It's too late to talk. You have to concentrate, I did my job already. Now it's your turn."

I changed my costume in the men's dressing room because there was no one around. Besides, I couldn't concentrate in the women's dressing room. Nancy Kerrigan had a bodyguard there, and Tonya Harding was there, plus the twenty-one other girls. Some of them had had good performances so they were laughing, and some had had bad ones so they were crying.

I was the third in my group. At the Worlds I had skated third in my group and at the Olympics I had skated third in my group. So, yes, I'm superstitious; that's a lucky number for me.

Since I had a little time, I took off my skates and I practiced jumping on the floor a little bit, and then I put my skates back on. I didn't see much of the two programs before mine, as I went to the ice just as Nancy was doing her last jump. She finished her program to a standing ovation. I went on the ice while people were still throwing flowers to her. I got really scared as I was skating around for the two minutes you have before you actually start. I remember the little girls picking up the flowers, and feeling my hair turn gray. Finally, the announcer gave my name and I went into the middle of the ice to start my program.

I didn't feel any pain. I didn't feel anything. I started with a combination jump, but I didn't do it like I was supposed to. So I changed my program totally. I was always doing that; it's just my personality. I would say the first half of it was Galina's choreography and the second half was my improvised choreography. I was going to do a triple toe loop but only did a double, so I was thinking, "I need a triple."

I was listening
to my boots—it's a little bit
cuckoo—
but I was listening
to the boots
and to the blades.
And I waited for
that moment,
when I would be ready,
when they would tell me,
"Oksana, you are ready,
you can start."
It was a voice
partly in my head,
and partly
up there in heaven.

So I tried another triple. I then threw in a triple toe and a combination jump. And before my program was over, I went for a double axel and a double toe loop and then, wait, my music is over, stop. I put my arms up. When I finished, I couldn't remember how I did it, I just remember that all the time something was clicking, clicking in my head:

"*Oh my God, I did it.*"

I was crying when I skated off the rink to wait for the scores. I was overwhelmed by everything — with all my trouble, and to still perform. Galina said, "Don't cry, don't cry. A lot of people are looking at you. You are going to go back into the dressing room and then you will cry there, but don't cry here. You have a lot of cameras in front of you."

Looking back at that moment, I realized that I never worried about the judges or the other skaters. I know some people say they have a good day or a bad day and that they don't care, that they just love to skate, but for me it's true. I really didn't worry about it, I just did what I had to do. And between my soul and God's soul, He knows the truth.

HE CAN TAKE
A LOT AWAY,
BUT HE
CAN
GIVE YOU
THAT
POWER.
THE POWER
THAT COMES
FROM
LOVING
WHAT YOU DO.

Conferring
with Galina
and Valentine
Nikolaj at
Lillehammer.

I didn't see anybody.

I was
never competing
at the
Olympic Games,
I didn't see
Nancy's
performance;
I just
didn't see it.
And I never
tried to compete
with anybody.
I just tried to
compete with myself.

They took me back into the dressing room, and I was sitting there, crying, thinking about my whole life: when I was young, when I first started skating, when I lied to my mom and she was harsh to me— all sorts of memories. After that I didn't watch the rest of the girls. I sat there crying and waiting. Galina came into the dressing room and said, "Well, I guess you are in third position." There were two more girls to skate. Surya Bonaly skated, and Galina came to say I was in second position. Not long after that, Galina opened the door again: "You win." I turned my head and I whispered to her, "I win?" I was in shock. At that moment the novocaine started wearing off, and I started feeling the pain.

I was crying and laughing a lot... I don't have a middle like other people do.

I was in pain, but I had to go to the podium.

I went to the make-up room and asked a girl to put a little makeup on my face,

but my tears kept falling down.

Then all the Russians came back—Victor, Sergei, Katya, Maia, Sasha—and they said,

"Moulya, you won!"

Getting Technical

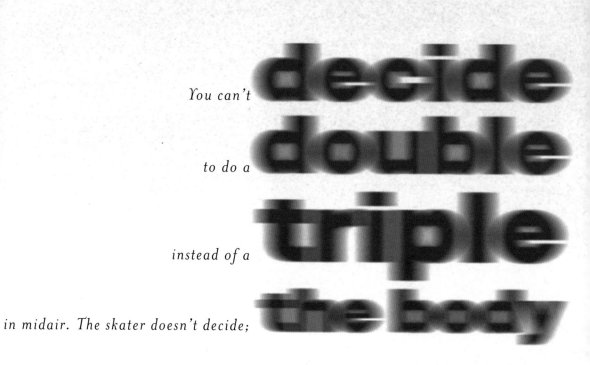

Jumps

AXEL

Take-off from a left forward outside edge, a counterclockwise rotation of one and a half revolutions in the air, and a landing on a right back outside edge. A **Double Axel** adds one rotation, and a **Triple Axel** adds two rotations.

SALCHOW

Take-off from a left back inside edge, one revolution counter-clockwise in the air, and a landing on a right back outside edge. **Double** and **Triple Salchows** add one and two revolutions, respectively.

LOOP

Take-off from a right back outside edge, one revolution counterclockwise in the air, and land on the same edge. Additional revolutions for the **Double Loop** and the **Triple Loop.**

You can't **decide** to do a **double** instead of a **triple** in midair. The skater doesn't decide; **the body**

It's not in the head, it's in

You can think before the jump and you can think after the jump, but

in the middle,

when you are rotating,

you can't see or think or feel.

Before the jump you are thinking about where

your head is

and where

your body is,

and after that it is sort of automatic,

like a machine. But things can happen.

A clock doesn't have a heart,

and people understand that

skaters are not clocks

or machines.

*We really don't care who does the best jumps,
because you can jump really **high**, but then after that you can **fall**,
and it means nothing. That means it was a triple salchow
and a fall. We are not measuring how **long** the jump is or how **high***

*it is, it's just a triple salchow—you take off on one edge, you rotate three
times, and you land on another edge—*

that is the jump.

*I was skating for Galina once, doing a
triple salchow, and I did what I thought was a fast and powerful one and she said,
"That's okay, but you made a mistake with your head
and you made a mistake with your arm."
And after that I did what I thought was an okay triple salchow, but she said,
"That's a great salchow*

because everything is all together,
like one piece."

1 2 3

TOE LOOP

A loop jump with a left toe-assisted take-off. Take-off from the right back outside edge, a left toe assist, one revolution counterclockwise in the air, and land on the right back outside edge. Additional revolutions for the **Double Toe Loop** and **Triple Toe Loop.**

FLIP

Take-off from the left back inside edge with a right toe assist, one revolution counter-clockwise in the air, landing on the right back outside edge. Additional revolutions for the **Double Flip** and **Triple Flip.**

LUTZ

Take-off from the left back outside edge, a right toe-pick assist, one revolution counter-clockwise in the air, landing on the right back outside edge. Additional revolutions for **Double Lutz** and **Triple Lutz.**

THE QUAD

At the 1997 Worlds, in Lausanne, Elvis Stojko completed the most difficult jump ever performed in competition: a **Quadruple Toe Loop** into **a Triple Toe Loop.** He was also the first to complete a quad combination in international competition when he performed a **Quadruple Toe Loop, Double Toe Loop** at the 1991 Worlds in Munich.

The jumps happen so fast; you take off and then you're down. You don't see yourself. You know the timing in the air. You don't really count; you just know the time of it so well. It's like something you have worked on so much, it becomes like a habit.

— MICHELLE KWAN

My favorite jump is the triple lutz. It is the hardest jump of the triples. I first did that when I was, say, twelve years old. In fact, that was my first triple. The axels I hate. I never did a triple axel. The axel is a really weird jump, and I hate doing it when my blade is really sharp, especially when you have to skate on a lot of different ices. You need to know the ice you are on really well when you are doing that jump.

When I was fifteen years old, I could jump easily. Then my body started changing and I couldn't jump so well anymore, but I also realized that figure skating is not just jumping.

Michelle Kwan

Tara Lipinski

Brian Boitano

Surya Bonaly

I do all the major jumps
except the triple axel. I
guess it's just really hard.
Midori Ito and Tonya
Harding are the only ones
that did it, but most
girls don't do it. I tried to
do a quad once, but I've
not really been practicing
it. If my coach decided
he wants to work on it
then I'm up to it.
— *TARA LIPINSKI*

Rudy Galindo

Elvis Stojko

The problem in
amateur skating
is that they
go overboard with
the triples;
they do **7** or **8**.
You don't need that,
but I do think
you need **3** or **4**.
— *E.M. SWIFT*

Sometimes you trip or fall,
it just happens.
You never know when you are going to die,
so in skating you
never know when you are going to fall. You just don't know.

When I fall down

I don't feel like I did something wrong.

So what.

Actually, I love to fall, because I can feel where my body is,

where my legs are,

where my arms are,

where my butt is.

Oomph.

Spins

SIT SPIN

A spin in a sitting position with the skating leg fully bent and the free leg extended forward and turned out, with the back slightly rounded.

CAMEL SPIN

A spin with the skating leg straight and the free leg extended straight back, parallel to the ice, with toe pointed, the back arched, and chin up at the same level as the free boot.

LAYBACK SPIN

From the forward upright spin, the torso is tilted back and the chest raised. The free leg is held at a 45-degree angle, turned out from the hip, the knee slightly lifted, and the lower leg parallel to the ice.

It took me two months to learn my special spin...

I was born without one vertebra in my back. I didn't know this until I was injured and I went for X-rays on my back before the Olympics. It gives me a lot of flexibility. But it causes me problems, too.

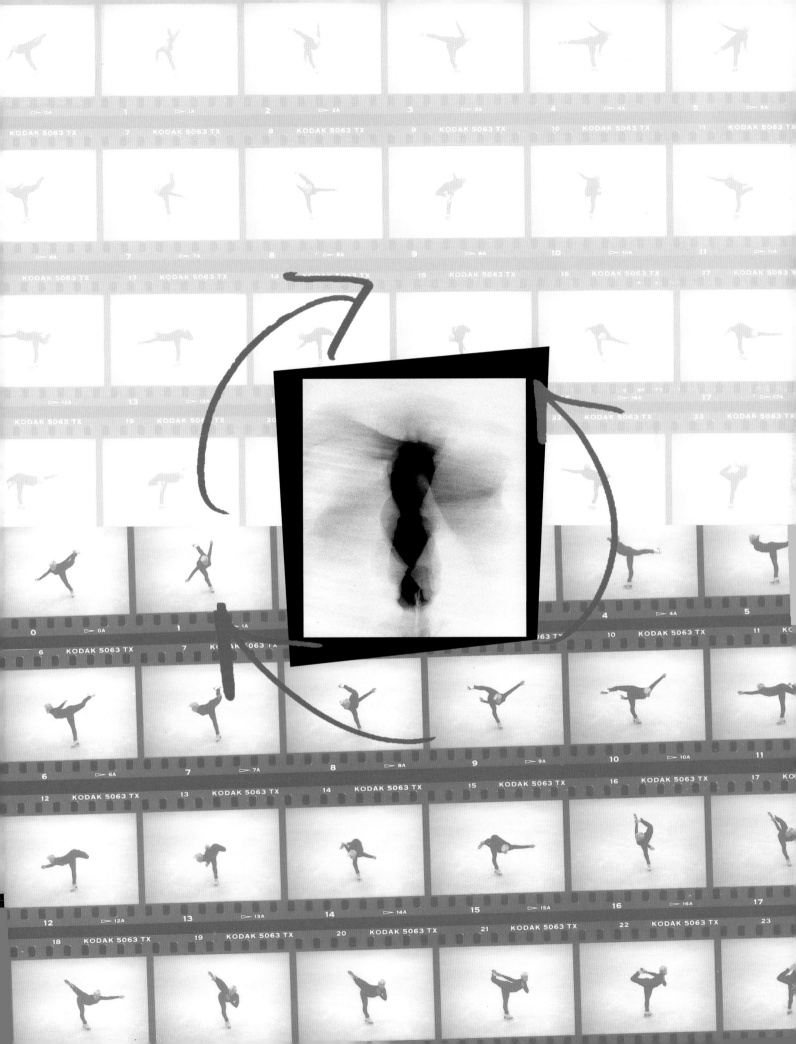

It's a blur wheN I am spinning. When you find your axis using your legs and arms, and you start to tighten up and pull them in, you go faster and faster. But after lots of practice you find your balance. When you find your axis using your legs and arms, sometimes I would get so dizzy I would fall down. Sometimes I would get so dizzy doing spins. I used to get dizzy doing spins.

When I come out of a spin, sometimes

I have to check and see

where I am and

where I have to go.

SPINS CONTINUED

FLYING CAMEL SPIN

Take-off from a left forward outside edge rotating about one revolution in the air and landing in a **Back Camel Spin.**

FLYING SIT SPIN

Take-off from a left forward outside edge assuming a sit spin position in the air while rotating about one and a half revolutions in the air and landing in a **Forward Sit Spin.**

DEATH DROP

Take-off from a left forward outside edge, the body horizontal to the ice in the air, face down, landing on a right back outside edge in a **Basic Sit Spin.**

ANATOMY OF A

IN THE FREE PROGRAM AT LILLEHAMMER I DID THE MUSIC FROM SWAN LAKE. IT WAS A LITTLE BIT DIFFERENT FROM MOST PROGRAMS, BECAUSE I WAS DANCING ON MY TOES. GALINA AND A BALLET CHOREOGRAPHER, NINA STOYAN, HAD STARTED WORKING TOGETHER. SINCE NINA WAS FROM BALLET THEATER, SHE DIDN'T KNOW MUCH ABOUT SKATING. SHE ASKED WHY I COULD NOT BE ON MY TOES ON THE ICE. I STARTED SCREAMING THAT IT WAS IMPOSSIBLE TO DO THAT, THAT NOBODY HAD EVER DONE IT BEFORE, AND THAT I DIDN'T WANT TO RISK IT. BUT THEY KEPT TELLING ME, "YES, YOU CAN DO IT, YOU CAN DO IT, IT'S NOT A BIG DEAL."

The ballerina's ankle has full range of motion.

The arch of the shoe is constructed to mold to the dancer's foot.

Balsa wood provides a firm base for balancing on toes.

Getting Technical

BALLET FOR THE ICE

Boot structure does not allow the performer to extend fully from arch to ankle.

Blade attached at arch limits a skater's ability to mimic the ballerina.

SO, OF COURSE, I DID SOME BALLET STEPS ON MY TOES. I KEPT TRYING, BUT MY LEGS WERE KILLING ME AND I COULDN'T STRAIGHTEN MY FOOT OUT. IT WAS REALLY HARD TO DO. NINA WOULD DANCE ON THE FLOOR, AND I WOULD TRY TO COPY HER ON THE ICE. GALINA WAS LOOKING AT ME AND THE CHOREOGRAPHER AND SHE WAS SAYING, "OH, I LIKE THAT STEP, LET'S GO PUT THAT TOGETHER. OH, I LIKE THAT MOVE, WE WILL TRY TO PUT THAT TOGETHER." AND THAT'S HOW WE CAME UP WITH THE PROGRAM.

Rules, Rules, Rules...

In competition, you perform the short and long programs. The short program is two and a half minutes long, and counts for thirty-three percent of the total score. The short program has required elements, and usually the top skaters have exact short programs with all the required elements in place...

And if you make a little mistake, you're down.

There are some required elements in the long program, but it's kind of all up to you.

—*MICHELLE KWAN*

The original program at Lillehammer had 8 required elements. Also, you can only wear certain costumes. You can't wear a lot of beading, a lot of glittery stuff, things like that. They have so many rules. And you can't make any mistake

Ever since they eliminated compulsory figures, the champions have been getting younger and younger.

The advantage of youth in most skaters, almost all skaters, is in their jumping ability.

But then they tend to lack something in the artistry because of their age.

—*E. M. SWIFT*

Lillehammer Winter Games 1994

JUDGES

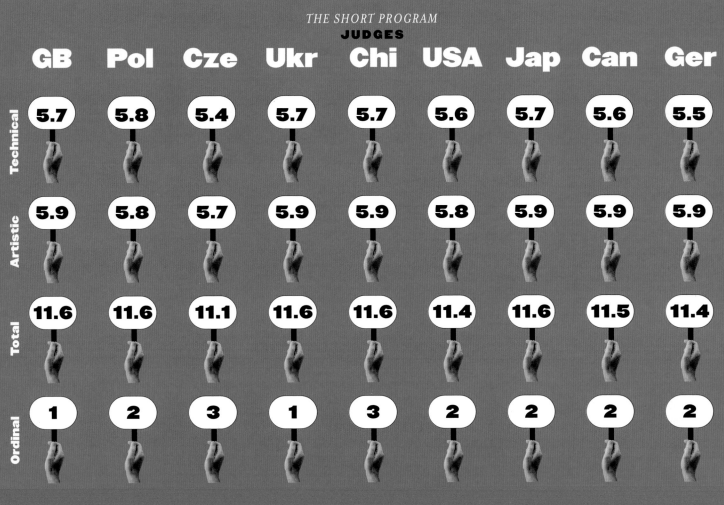

	GB	Pol	Cze	Ukr	Chi	USA	Jap	Can	Ger
Technical	5.7	5.8	5.4	5.7	5.7	5.6	5.7	5.6	5.5
Artistic	5.9	5.8	5.7	5.9	5.9	5.8	5.9	5.9	5.9
Total	11.6	11.6	11.1	11.6	11.6	11.4	11.6	11.5	11.4
Ordinal	1	2	3	1	3	2	2	2	2

THE LONG PROGRAM

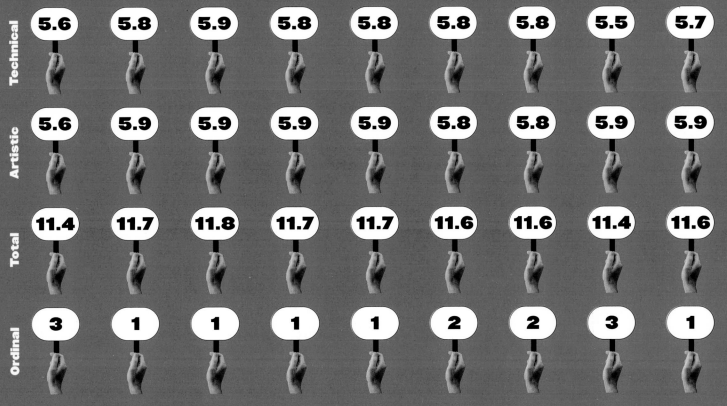

	GB	Pol	Cze	Ukr	Chi	USA	Jap	Can	Ger
Technical	5.6	5.8	5.9	5.8	5.8	5.8	5.8	5.5	5.7
Artistic	5.6	5.9	5.9	5.9	5.9	5.8	5.8	5.9	5.9
Total	11.4	11.7	11.8	11.7	11.7	11.6	11.6	11.4	11.6
Ordinal	3	1	1	1	1	2	2	3	1

Every sport needs rules...

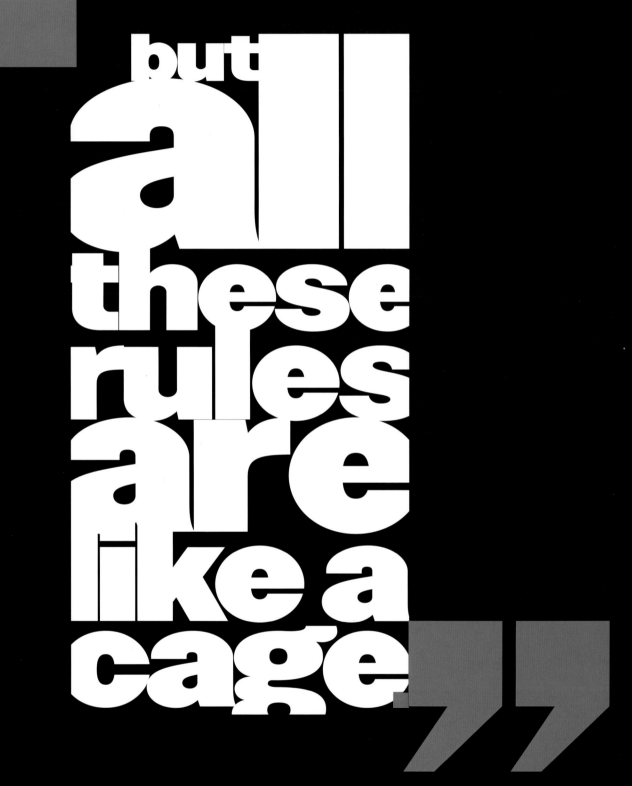

" but all these rules are like a cage "

5

Mastering the Art

I FEEL REALLY POWERFUL ON THE ICE. I HAVE TO FEEL POWERFUL. PEOPLE COME TO SEE ME AND I HAVE TO BE HAPPY AND SELF-CONFIDENT.

AS A PROFESSIONAL, I SKATE TO ENTERTAIN, BUT I STILL HAVE TO BE VERY GOOD. NOW THE AUDIENCE HELPS ME TO DO THAT. I AM OLDER NOW AND I AM BEGINNING TO UNDERSTAND MY- SELF MORE THAN I USED TO. AND I DON'T THINK MY PERSONALITY IS JUST ABOUT COMPETING WITH SOMEBODY. PROFESSIONAL FIGURE SKATING ALLOWS ME TO DO WHAT I LIKE BEST: JUST GOING OUT ON THE ICE AND PERFORMING.

Jumping is how many skaters judge themselves these days. And the young skaters begin to create tougher and tougher standards. Now you have the quadruple jump. What's next? After a while, I said to myself, "Okay, I can't jump like I used to, but what kind of numbers should I do for people to keep them interested in my figure skating?"

The "Nutcracker on Ice," 1995, with Brian Boitano

If you have a library,
you don't want a hundred
copies of the same book.
No — you want a hundred
different books. It is the
same way with my
skating repertoire: I want all
sorts of different performances.

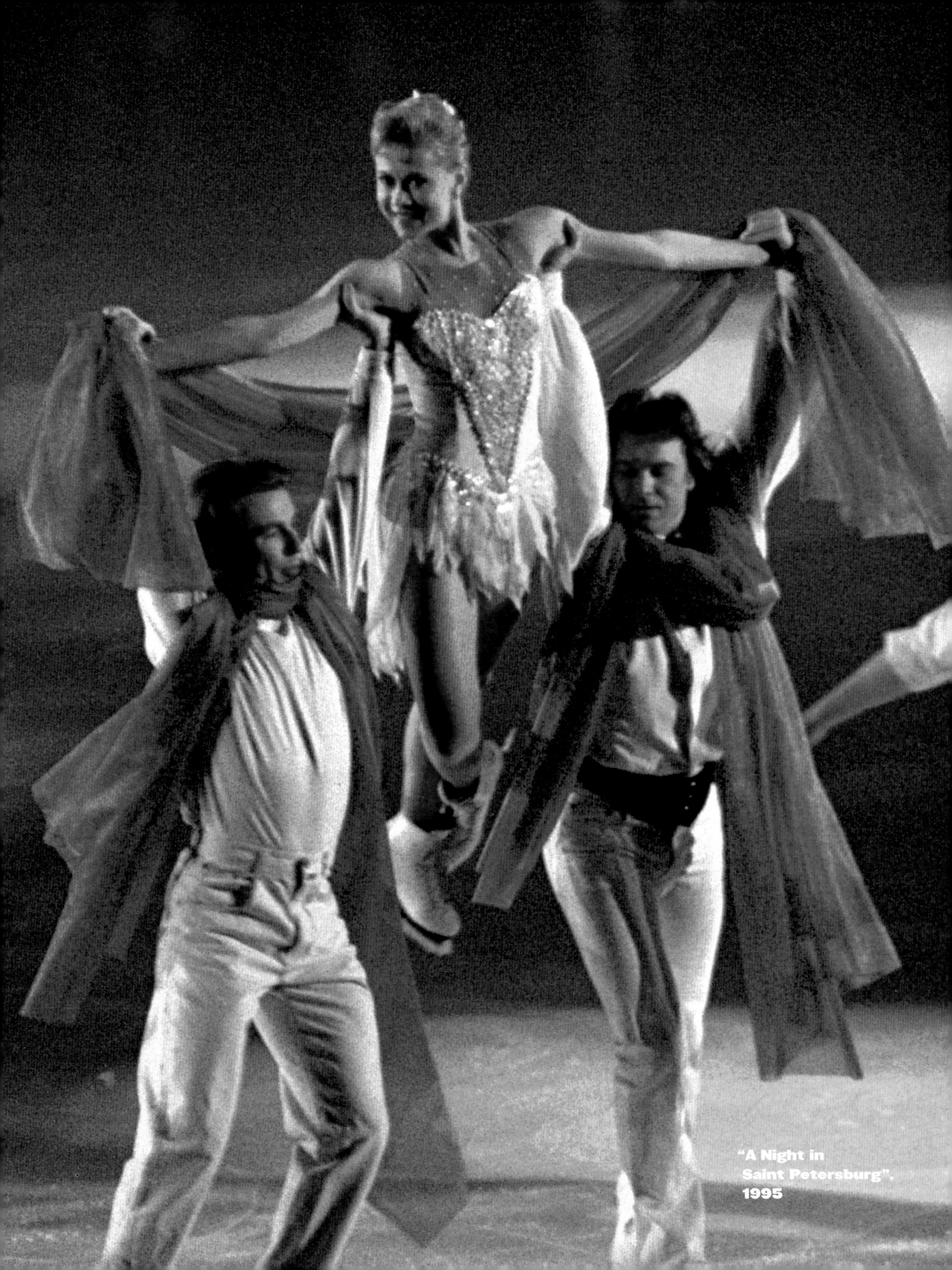

"A Night in
Saint Petersburg",
1995

I want people

to think of me

as an artist.

I don't want people

to think of me

as an athlete.

Of course,

skating is athletic,

but it is also

graceful,

more expressive,

especially in the shows.

Professional skating

is about
expressing
yourself.

**First night,
1997 Tom
Collins Tour**

Skating is not like track & field.

It's not the running. It's not the jumping. Because jumpers have to jump as far as they can or as high as they can. That is their goal, what they have to do.

In professional
figure skating,
you don't
have to jump
as far or as high as you can.
They are
not measuring that;
they are judging

the whole thing:
spins, steps, jumps—

everything

together.

ON
6
TOUR

On The Bus:
The Tom
Collins 1996
Tour of
World Figure
Skating
Champions

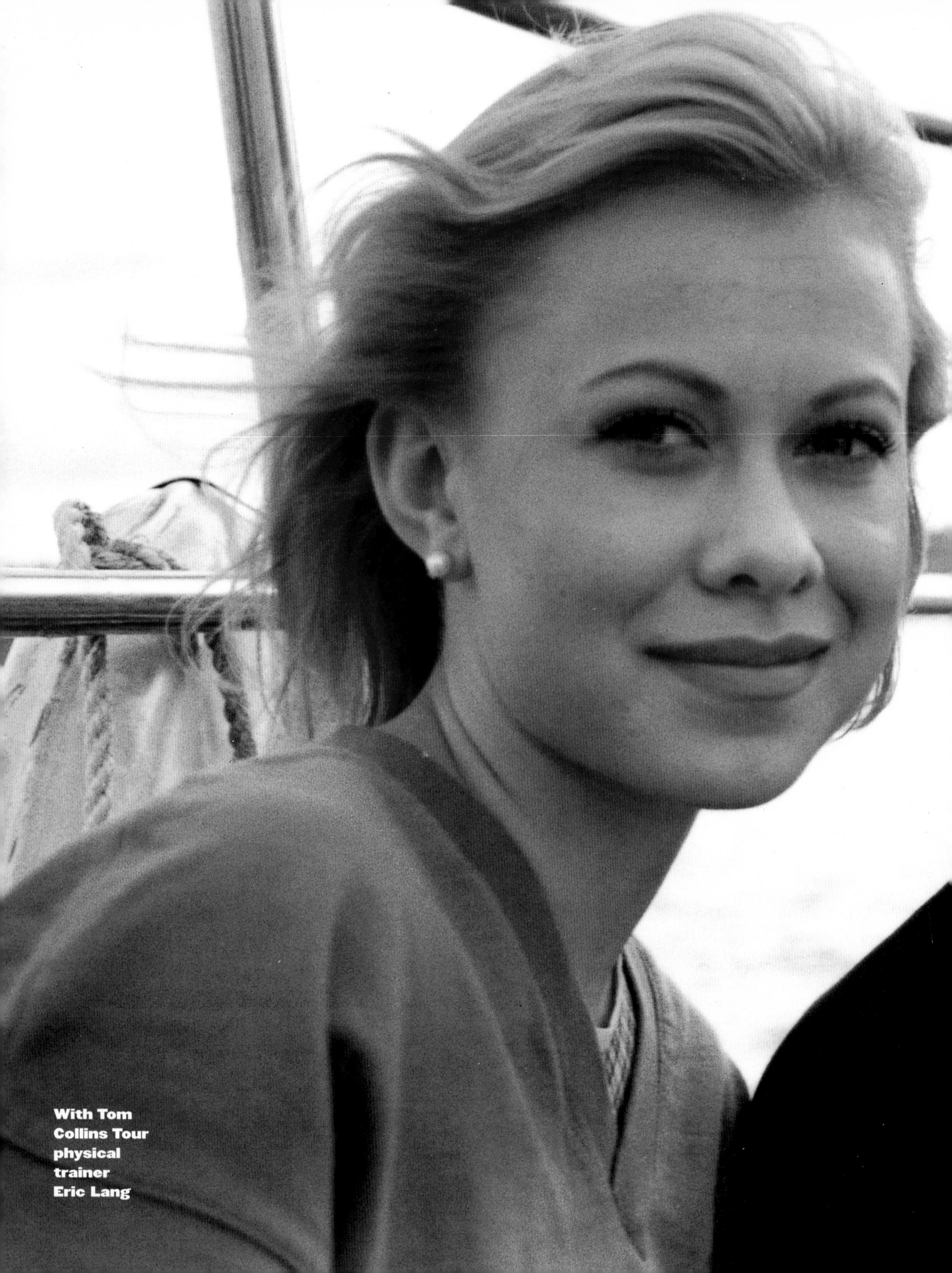

With Tom Collins Tour physical trainer Eric Lang

"Ice Fishing"
on The 1995 Tour,
with Nancy Kerrigan,
Michelle Kwan
and Brian Boitano.

When I step out on the ice I can be really nervous; that's the moment before I have to start skating, but after the music starts, after a couple of seconds, I forget everything. I am just skating with the music. It's so much better to skate than to watch somebody else's performance.

It isn't easier as a professional. I guess it depends on what you want from life or from skating. I still get nervous. Because when I go on the ice, I have to make sure that I am inspiring people enough that they might even fall in love with my skating. I have to be expressive. And that can be really hard to do, especially on the ice. You have to have a really close connection with the audience. When I was an amateur, it was different, because I was more concerned about skating the perfect routine and that the judges would give me good marks.

Sometimes when I am skating in the dark with the spotlights, and I can see only the first couple of rows, I suddenly see their eyes. At that moment, I can tell if they are interested or not.

Even with
all the friends and company,
touring is lonely
and tiring—
a different city every night.
Most nights,
I go back to the hotel
and
go to sleep,
just waiting for the next chance
to get back
on the ice.

Putting It All Together

From the first costume sketch, to the fittings, to the music and choreography... It all must come together.

The Costume:

*I usually have
three costumes for a show—*
**for the opening,
the number,
and the closing.**
*It depends on the show.
For "Nutcracker," I had five
or six costumes.
Each one takes a lot of work:*
design,
the right materials,
**dressmaking,
fitting—
everything.**

Dress Fitting, New York, 1997, with Alina Panova (left) and Barbara Matera (center)

On Costumes

skirt · 6·8 petals
petals painting
sheer

Alina Panova
1997

OKSANA BAIUL
FLOWER dRESS

#4

Alina Panova: Designing for the Ice

Ballet is close to figure skating. In both cases the costumes need to be light and flowing. But in figure skating you have an additional element: It is both an art and a sport. When a skater makes triple jumps, she can't get caught up in her dress in the middle of a rotation. There are a lot of things like that a designer has to think about.

At the same time figure skating gives beautiful lines to the costumes, because the speed of the skater extends the costume. You can never create that in dance, unless a ballerina is being carried by a male dancer.

In ballet you can use fantastic natural fabrics, especially silk, and in figure skating it used to be the same. But now most people don't use natural fabrics because they get destroyed on the ice.

The stage in ballet is usually a proscenium, with preset lighting and a fixed perspective, with the audience on one side and the performers on the other. In figure skating the arenas are huge and people are looking from all directions. Most of the time the lighting is unpredictable. You can create the most beautiful costume, but it will be lit differently in each arena. And the costume will either disappear or will look totally different from the design.

The costume has to read from a very great distance. But at the same time I have to think about television,

with all its tight close-ups. I try to accommodate two opposite perspectives. With Oksana's costume for the 1994 tour, the flower costume, the bodice was a corset made with a special type of soft bone that is firm but flexible. I needed to make the bodice early on, so she could break it in, a little bit like shoes. It looks amazing, like it is molded to her body.

The bodice is basically designed like a swimming suit, with the skirt on top. I would visit the rehearsals and pin little samples of different fabrics to Oksana to see which ones flowed better. And then we started adjusting the length and doing the petals for the flower costume.

SKATING
dress of sheer
BLK net (top) +
chiffon (skirt) w/
pane velvet
bodice. reembroid—

- Pale Blue shiffon
the WAIST, n—

- HEAVIER Beading th
torso + then slowly
disappearing in
nothing at Skirt

When we decided on the final sketch, I brought it to Barbara Matera (a renowned theatrical dressmaker), and we discussed the structure. Since there are so many ways the dress can be executed based on the basic design, it normally takes about two months to have it made. Then we have fittings. And it's always a work in progress. You are constantly readjusting. While it's not exactly fashion, pieces like the flower costume are often done in a couture tradition. But above all, the costume has a function, and there are so many purposes to serve in addition to looking pretty.

SOMETIMES

YOU HAVE AN AMAZING IDEA: YOU ARE PLAYING THE RADIO IN THE CAR, ENJOYING THE MUSIC, AND SUDDENLY IT HITS YOU.

WHEN I WATCH  MOVIES OR LISTEN TO MUSIC I AM THINKING OF MY NUMBERS. WHEN I WAS YOUNGER, GALINA WOULD CHOOSE MUSIC FOR ME, AND WHEN I GOT A LITTLE OLDER, WE WERE SELECTING PIECES TOGETHER, DECIDING WHAT WE LIKED, WHAT I WOULD SKATE TO. NOW I ALWAYS CHOOSE THE MUSIC FOR MYSELF.

Putting it All Together

Music has to be very carefully

coordinated—every note is like a cue.

For "Night in
Saint Petersburg,"

it was really hard

for all of us because

we were skating to

live music

with the orchestra.

And all the time the conductor was playing the music

a little bit faster,

a little bit slower.

Usually you are working

with music on tape

and you don't have to worry

about the timing.

My style is not very "rock and roll," but more classical. In my 1997 program, the flower piece, I used music from Beethoven's Symphony No. 8. I "discovered" it while watching the movie Immortal Beloved *with Isabella Rosellini and Gary Oldman. I was watching the film, and when I heard that beautiful piece, I thought, "Sara, I've found the music!"*

It's really hard to find music for skating because people have already used a lot of famous pieces.

**Choreographer
Sara Kawahara**

I usually work
with classical music for
competitions, but
something that is still
practical and powerful.
It's better for the judges
and it's easier to skate
to. It lets you flow more
and show more character.
You know it's hard to
find the right piece, but
you eventually do.

—*TARA LIPINSKI*

When you choreograph, you create a vocabulary of technical elements. In order to create new movement you have to have decent technique in your skating. You have to know where the center is in that the program will come to life and blossom; to do that, the skater has to train diligently. That's the only way that art is justified within skating: if there is fusion. I never choreograph a with them. And that way it is given life by both of us together. For a professional, skating requires a very intelligent dialog. Up to that point in their lives skaters have been directed; every

order to move away from it—just like in ballet. So there is technique wherever you go; you can't run away from it: figure skating is an art form—but it's a sport first. When I create a program I want to know that the skater will follow through. I want to know

With Tai Babilonia and Sara

piece for an individual skater without the skater present. And when I work with individuals, I like to know what they feel, or what their take is. I then come up with my own ideas, we work together, and I create the number iota of their soul has been directed and trained. Only after they turn professional do they have a chance to spread their wings and get to know who they are and to use the tools and the positioning that they have acquired to say something else.

—*SARA KAWAHARA*

Sharp Like a Needle:

If you want to learn, you need a lot of people to give you inspiration to help you develop different programs. A coach and a choreographer have two different roles. A coach is the person who helps you with your jumps, with your physical training, getting ready for competitions. The choreographer is the person who helps with new programs, costumes, lighting, and the show. Unlike competition, you don't perform once or twice a year, you do it every night in a different city, in front of a new audience each time. When you go out on the ice, you have your make-up done, you have your hair done, and you have your costume and music. Everything must be sharp like a needle. It has to be perfect. What if you were to see a musical on Broadway and Beauty—or the Beast—is without a proper costume or the right make-up. So it is with figure skating.

116

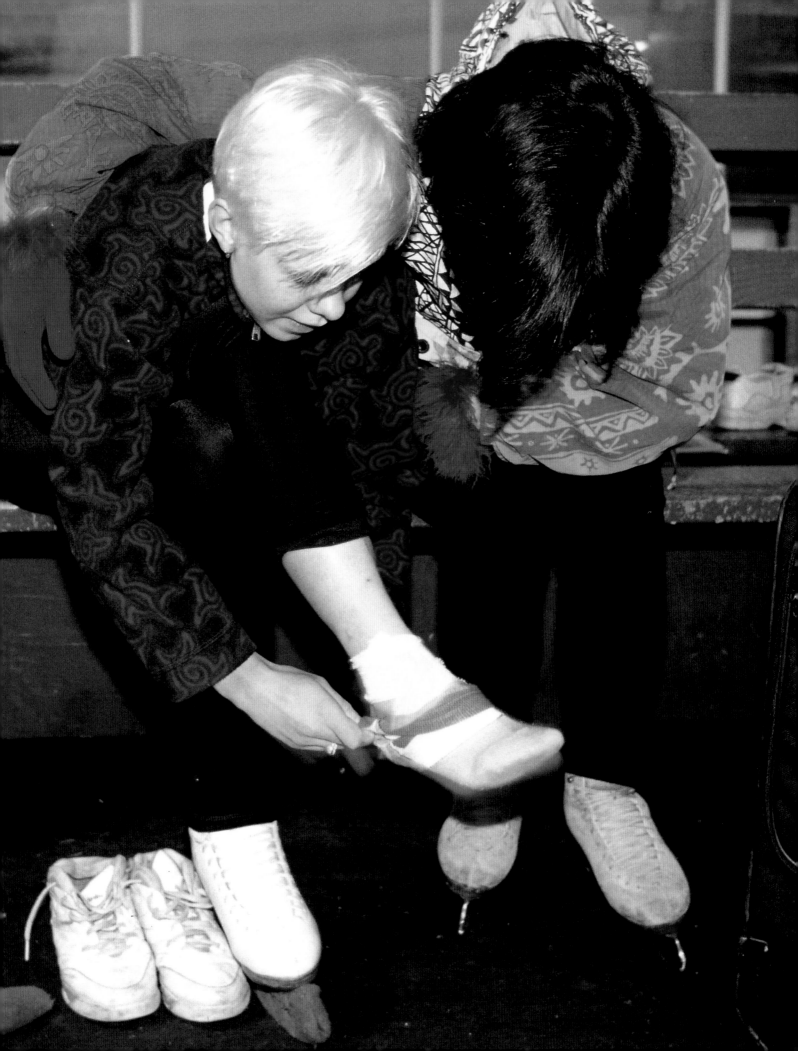

With Tai
Babilonia

A Winning Program:

In 1992 at the Olympics I knew I had a good program. Galina, with the choreographer, explained the music, the movements, and the story of the music. I read related books and literature to understand the depth of the performance.

We set the piece on the floor in the dance room without skates to see how the number would work. We put the skating elements in the plan and connected them to figure skating steps and movements. At the same time, I was continuing to work on skating technique. Then we would watch it on video and work through it with the choreographer. Slowly it grows into a full number. Then you correct the steps, the movements, and it is ready.

— *VICTOR PETRENKO*

In training I do everything: I work in the gym, I run, I work on flexibility, and I take ballet when I can.

Water therapy at the Burdenko Institute

You have to focus on different parts of your body on different days. Sometimes, your legs are stiff so you have to work them up a little bit more. I usually start out by running a little bit in the corridor, and then I start warming up my head and neck and then shoulders and arms, legs, ankles, and finally toes and fingers. When I have been traveling a lot, I have to warm up my body a little more.

While I am warming up I am thinking about my program. After warming up my body, I start jumping a little, just to feel it, and then I "skate" my program on the floor. I see myself skating, especially the jumps. And then I stretch a little bit. I don't stretch too much because I don't want to get too loose. Its not good to be too loose. You could hurt yourself.

You have to work around
your injuries
and still
stay in shape.
If your back is feeling
a little bit better,
your ankle starts hurting.
If your ankle feels
a little bit better,
your head starts
hurting.
That's a
skater's life.

Style

I am no longer trying to learn specifically from other skaters because I think every skater has their own style. That's their private thing, especially at this level of skating. I can't imagine stealing from them, because they're all my friends. But I like it when kids learn from me. That's different.

When you are an amateur you start to find your style, but mostly you are thinking like this: "Okay, today I am going to do this program. Tomorrow I am going to do the same program, and the day after tomorrow I am going to do that program again. Until I've perfected that single routine." Professionals, however, must have a whole collection of programs. And every single number has to be interesting. Competitive amateurs often can only think about medals. Skaters should think about art, about soul.

Too often
people are repeating
what's

been done before.
A great performance
starts in the

skater's heart
and gets
mapped out
from there.

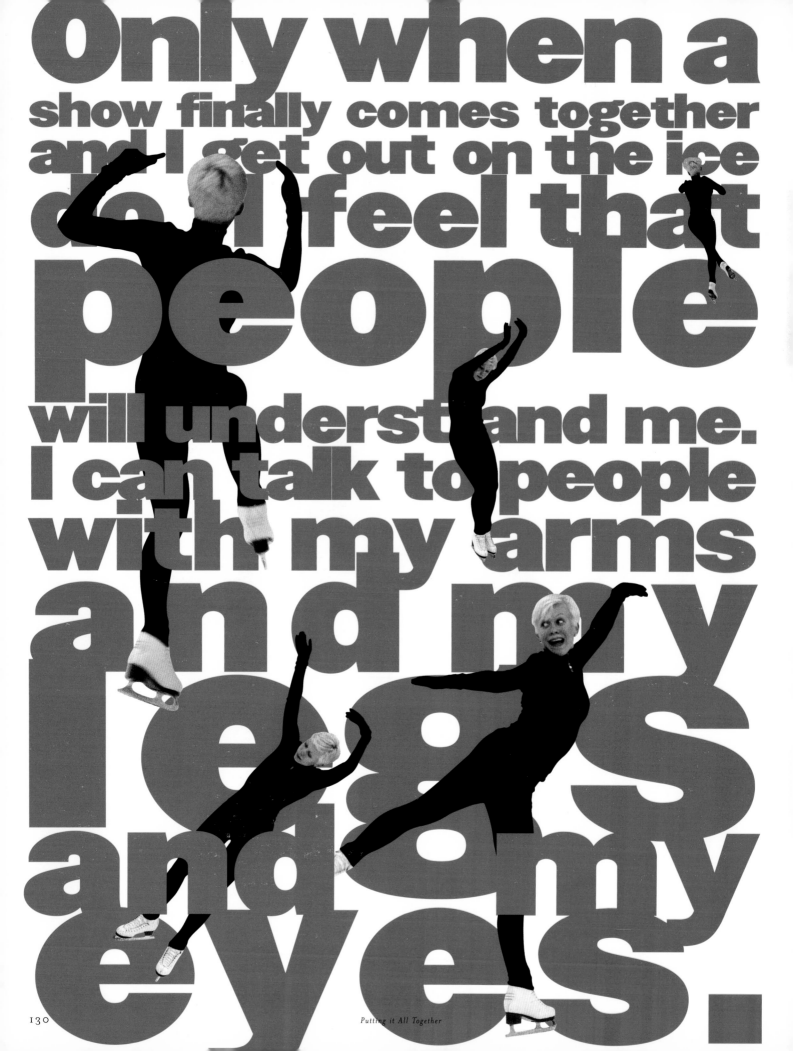

Only when a show finally comes together and I get out on the ice do I feel that people will understand me. I can talk to people with my arms and my legs and my eyes.

I can
tell them
anything
I like.

Lessons

8

Hard Lessons

Figure skating, I discovered very quickly, is a very intense life—with very high highs and some very low lows. When I had a car accident, I had been working straight for three years without a vacation.

When you are a figure skater you can have such a small circle. You can find yourself in a cage, thinking only about figure skating. My other friends were eating as much as they wanted, and they could go out and party until three o'clock in the morning. For me it was different.

I think I had that car accident because I got to the point where I was taking time off only for moments at a time—and in the wrong way. I felt so much pressure, so responsible to the audience. I would tell myself, I have to skate and skate and skate. I got to the point where I had so many commitments but could still not say no. I reached the point where I didn't want to skate anymore. For a while, I didn't think I would go back to the ice. I had burned out.

After my car accident, a good friend of mine said to me, "Did you see the blood in the back seat. Why didn't God take your life? It was a wake-up call. He hates to see you throw your life away. He gave you such a talent. He gave you so many good people around you. If you can't learn from somebody else's mistakes you have to learn from your own".

About three months after the accident I said to myself, "Something is missing in my life. I don't understand why I am so miserable. I have to go back on the ice." So I did, and I was so happy. I had forgotten I was an Olympic champion and that I had worked hard for that medal. That's why I went back to the ice rink; that's why I said to myself,

I want to work again. I just have to feel the ice under my feet.

Life sometimes has harsh ways of teaching you, but learning is the essence of life. When I went on the ice after the car accident, my body was different, I had gained weight and I didn't feel right. I felt like I had my boots on the wrong feet. I had lost that sense of myself.

I've had to start teaching myself again. The old system of learning worked for a while, but eventually you need a new approach. In the past, I had a system: I had to do a hundred jumps and then be sure I landed a percentage of those jumps. But right now I am not like that. I am saying to myself I have to do two or three jumps, and I have to land them all. I have to picture them in my head and I know I am going to do them. Of course, sometimes I fall; sometimes you do have to make mistakes.

I love professional figure skating. I won some medals and people started recognizing me. I became a professional figure skater because I didn't want to be a sports person anymore. I wanted to be an artist. Now, I am free to learn something new.

Not a lot of people **get to be** **champions.** *Of course, it is amazing if you do. But I think* **in figure skating,** *you can still* **express yourself** *even if you don't win any medals. You have to work* **very hard** *to give yourself the chance, you have to suffer a lot, but will you* **be happy** *if you don't try?*

Photography

1: Simon Bruty 2–3: Simon Bruty 4–5: Simon Bruty 6–7: Tony Duffy/Allsport 9: Gérard Vandystadt/Allsport 10–11: Simon Bruty 12: Simon Bruty 13: (clockwise from top left): Courtesy Oksana Baiul / Gérard Vandystadt/Allsport / Simon Bruty / Simon Bruty / Simon Bruty / Simon Bruty / Simon Bruty / Simon Bruty / Allsport 14: Todd Eberle 15: Gérard Châtaigneaux 16: Courtesy Oksana Baiul 17: Courtesy Oksana Baiul 18: Courtesy Oksana Baiul 19: Courtesy Oksana Baiul 20: Courtesy Oksana Baiul 21: Courtesy Oksana Baiul 22–23: Courtesy Oksana Baiul 24: Courtesy Oksana Baiul 25: Gérard Vandystadt/Allsport 26: Gérard Vandystadt/Allsport 27: F. Scott Grant 29: Gérard Vandystadt/Allsport 30: Courtesy Oksana Baiul 31: Courtesy Oksana Baiul 32: Gérard Vandystadt/Allsport 34 (inset): F. Scott Grant 34 (bottom): Todd Eberle 35: Focus on Sports 36: Gérard Vandystadt/Allsport 37: Anton Want/Allsport 38–39: Courtesy Oksana Baiul 40: Gérard Vandystadt/Allsport 42: Simon Bruty 45: F. Scott Grant 46: F. Scott Grant 47: Tony Duffy/Allsport 48–49: F. Scott Grant 51: Mike Powell/Allsport 52–53: Simon Bruty 54–55: Simon Bruty 56 (left): Simon Bruty 56–57 (center): Gérard Vandystadt/ Allsport 56–57 (bottom): Courtesy Guepard Productions International 58 (Kwan/Bonaly/Baiul): Simon Bruty 58 (Lipinski): Stu Foster/Allsport 58 (Boitano): Mike Powell/Allsport 59 (Galindo/Baiul): Simon Bruty 59 (Stojko): Stu Foster/Allsport 60–61: Simon Bruty 62: Simon Bruty 63: Simon Bruty 64: Claus Andersen 65 (clockwise from top): Simon Bruty / Duomo— David Madison / Simon Bruty / Simon Bruty 66: Bruce Byers/ FPG Int'l 67: Simon Bruty 70: Tony Duffy/Allsport 72–73: Simon Bruty 74: Simon Bruty 75: Michelle Harvath 77: Gérard Vandystadt/Allsport 78–79: Simon Bruty 80: Simon Bruty 81: Paul Harvath 82–83: Courtesy Oksana Baiul 84–85: Simon Bruty 86–87: Courtesy Oksana Baiul 88–89: Courtesy Oksana Baiul 90: Courtesy Oksana Baiul 91: Richard Martin/Allsport 92–93: Simon Bruty 94–95: Simon Bruty 96–97: Simon Bruty 98–99: Simon Bruty 100–101: Simon Bruty 102: Courtesy Alina Panova 103: Courtesy Alina Panova 104–105: Simon Bruty 106: Simon Bruty 107: Gérard Vandystadt/Allsport 108: Simon Bruty 109: Simon Bruty 110–111: Simon Bruty 112–113: Simon Bruty 114: Simon Bruty 115: Simon Bruty 116: Simon Bruty 117: Simon Bruty 118: Simon Bruty 119: Paul Harvath 120–121: Simon Bruty 122: Courtesy The Burdenko Institute 123: Courtesy The Burdenko Institute 124: Simon Bruty 125: Simon Bruty 126: Daniela Federici 127: Simon Bruty 128–129: Simon Bruty 130: Simon Bruty 131: Simon Bruty 132: Simon Bruty 134–135: Simon Bruty 136–137: Daniela Federici 138–139: Simon Bruty 140–141: Simon Bruty 142: Simon Bruty 143: Simon Bruty 144: Simon Bruty

Thanks to
Galina Zmievskaya,
Victor, Nina,
Sarah Kawahara,
Alina Panova, Barbara Matera,
Michael and Shelly
and the
William Morris Agency,
Maia, Jodi,
Brian Boitano,
and Eric Lang,
and the
Tom Collins Tour.
Special thanks
to Christopher,
Simon Bruty,
Charles Miers,
David McAninch,
Alex Isley, Kim Okosky,
and all my
true friends
and fans.